Martial Arts UNLOCKED

Martial Arts UNLOCKED

A Parent's Guide for Choosing a Martial Arts School

Joseph Ash

Advantage®

Published by Advantage, Charleston, South Carolina.

Member of Advantage Media Group.
ADVANTAGE is a registered trademark and the Advantage colophon is a trademark of

Advantage Media Group, Inc.
Printed in the United States of America.

ISBN: 978-159932-406-7
LCCN: 2013933421

PREFACE

To Parents

Congratulations on making the decision to pursue martial-arts education for your child and/or family. An investment of this type will be extremely rewarding on many levels. It is my intent to help you along the way in selecting the ideal program for you and your family.

It is likely that, at some point, your child will want to take a martial-arts course because of something he saw in a movie or because of a friend's request. Then, like every good parent, you will begin researching. When this happens, where do you start and what do you ask? Perhaps you start by looking on the Internet for random ideas about martial arts. You find a few sites in your area and begin to read about them while stumbling over several terms ending in *-do*, *-jiujitsu*, or *-chi*. But do you even know what those mean?

Then, you will narrow down your search to a select few schools based on what the sites look like or maybe even some nicely written copy. Nowadays, with the Internet flooded with information about the arts, this material is not hard to find. After that, you have an interview with an instructor or call the school, and 90 percent or more of that interaction is based upon what you have just learned. After you use all that information up, you are at the mercy of a school owner, salesperson, or program director. From this point forward, a school's representative can lead you down the rabbit hole; alternatively, if you're lucky, he or she will give you a better understanding of what it is the school provides and how its representatives can help.

Beginning your research for a martial-arts school can be a bit overwhelming. The media is constantly drawing attention to the wrong areas of sports, news, and public information. Given this, how do you know what, when, and where to look for quality information? There are so many resources and media portrayals regarding what martial arts is and how it should be taught, practiced, and used that, often, people take a shot in the dark. Doing so is not wrong; instead, what it means is that people just do not have enough information to search properly, and when they find something, they ask the wrong questions.

One of my biggest challenges as a martial-arts school owner and educator is helping people overcome their predispositions about martial arts, which can include their recent research or what they learned in the past under their own great grand master, master, or something similar. I have trudged long enough through less-than-favorable displays of martial-arts media, sporting events, and actual programs claiming fame based on one thing or another. Such outlandish claims not only do a great injustice to my fellow martial artists but are also unjust to you, the consumer, who may not know enough to choose the right program for your family. It is my sincere hope that the knowledge you gain from reading this book will lead you to the ideal program for your martial-arts education.

As a martial-arts professional, I can tell you with 100 percent certainty that there is no one school that will fit all people. I have written this book with the purest intention of educating people who may not have the benefit of a personal consultation with me to understand how martial-arts schools differ and how the business works. In this book, I will not be sharing knowledge about martial-arts styles or giving you a list of instructors who can perform the fastest side kicks. However, I will explain to you what I have learned after thirty-plus years spent in the martial arts (as a student, athlete, employee, teacher, and school owner); there are profound degrees of separation among martial-arts schools. This book is dedicated to arming people like you with better questions to ask when searching for your ideal school. After all, I believe you are not only choosing a school; you are choosing a whole support system for yourself and your family.

From my family to yours, enjoy.

To School Owners

In today's world of entertainment, news, and hearsay about what is and what isn't true, having a strong resource, such as this book, will prove valuable when educating your prospective martial-arts students. Whether you are calling prospects or meeting people at a community event, this book will serve as a helpful tool for your prospects in their quest for the ideal school, which, I hope, will be yours. This book will better educate them about the martial-arts business and standards I feel all professionals should share. Therefore, once they have this information, they will realize that other schools with subpar standards will not make the cut. In turn, this will raise the credibility of your program to new levels.

As a school owner myself, I know the necessity of maximizing both time and energy to be 100 percent focused on the members. This book is an excellent source for opening and directing your prospects' minds, allowing you to work with more focused, informed prospects. With a copy of this book in hand, new prospects can also feel more secure about their decision to train with you because of your openness and honesty about what your program stands for and can do for their families.

CHAPTER 1

MARTIAL-ARTS STYLES

Our family would like to extend a heartfelt thank-you for all you have done for us in the past five years. We knew what we were looking for in a martial-arts school, and our experience has far exceeded our expectations!

— *THE FRYE FAMILY*

Martial-Arts Style

Frequently, parents will call my school and ask if I teach a particular style of martial arts, such as tae kwon do, karate, kung fu, or jiujitsu. After a second or third question, it is obvious to me they have little or no idea why they are asking such a question. The point of this chapter is not to differentiate the styles or to sway your decision one way or the other. Instead, the point here is this: the particular kind of martial art is of little to no importance to the average individual and should not rank that highly in your decision-making process.

Most people's understanding of a style is limited to a friend's referral or some other form of marketing material. Magazines, movies, and, often, personal experience may play a role in influencing a person's choice of style. A referral is wonderful and, perhaps, one of the strongest indicators of a solid program.

However, it does not tell you about style. Instead, style comes down to the selection of teacher (which I will discuss later on in the book). There is no replacement for actual hands-on experience.

Since we are living in the twenty-first century, we have plenty of martial arts from which to choose. If you drive by any strip mall, you are likely to notice signs for "Joe's Tae Kwon Do," "Kim's Karate," or some other wording brightly lit up on the building's canopy. On the Internet, you will find there are exponentially more programs battling for your attention with high-end websites, freebies, and other catchy offers.

Such an abundance of information makes it extremely difficult for the average parent to find high-quality information about martial-arts education. The good side to all this is that schools providing each of the styles mentioned above can provide members with fitness, self-defense, discipline, and respect. These qualities are what I think of as natural byproducts of any good martial-arts program.

As you or your child's decision pertains to style, you should look into types of program in which you might wish to participate. Nowadays, it is more and more difficult to find specialty styles, such as the old

Snake and Crane Kung Fu we use to stumble upon as we flipped through the channels and caught *Black Belt Theater*. Even if you find such a school, the likelihood of it being truly what you are looking for is slim to none.

Almost every style you hear of has in some way or form developed from karate, tae kwon do, or kung fu. (Of course, there are exceptions.) There will always be examples of great teachers, such as Mr. Miyagi and the Cobra Kai instructors. Nevertheless, tae kwon do and karate tend to be more universal for both children and adults. Some well-structured programs are capable of working with entire families effectively.

• MASTER'S TIP •

If I had to choose, I would feel comfortable saying your best bet for finding what you are looking for would be at a professional school that teaches either tae kwon do or karate. These two arts have consistently been staples in the industry and are the most user-friendly in terms of both starting and sustaining members for longer periods of time, therefore providing greater long-term outcomes.

General descriptions of the some of the more popular Martial Art today

Tae Kwon Do: Originating from South Korea, it means the "way of the Foot and Hand." It is the most popular form of Martial Art practiced amongst families throughout the world and one of two Olympic Martial Art sports (as of this publication).

Karate: Literally means "empty hand" and originated in Okinawa, Japan. It contains the second largest population of Martial Artists.*

Kung Fu: Originating in China, and it's original meaning is any skill achieved through hard work or practice, not necessarily martial in nature.*

Judo: Tracing origins back to 1882, Judo means the "Gentle Way" and was created in Japan. It is the only other Martial Arts besides Tae Kwon Do in the Olympic Games (as of this publication)

Aikido: Meaning "the way of unifying with life." It began in Japan.

Hapkido: Meaning "the way of coordinating energy." It is similar to Aikido but from Korea.

Mixed Martial Arts: American buzz word meaning what it sounds like.

Ju Jutsu: Also originated in Japan, meaning the "Gentle Art." Ju Jutsu has spawned sports like Judo and Brazilian Jiu Jitsu.

Kendo: Originating in Japan meaning "the Way of the Sword."

Gum Do: Originating in Korea meaning "the Way of the Sword." Derived from Kendo – very similar in mechanics.

Muy Tai: A combat sport from Thailand that means the "Art of Eight Hands."

Tai Chi: A Chinese Martial Art, it means "Boundless Fist."

**There are many different sub-styles types of Karate and Kung Fu. Try to find the most purest forms that fit your family needs if you choose one of these styles.*

Note: All sources above was taken from the same Wikipeida resource.

CHAPTER 2

SCHOOL GENRES

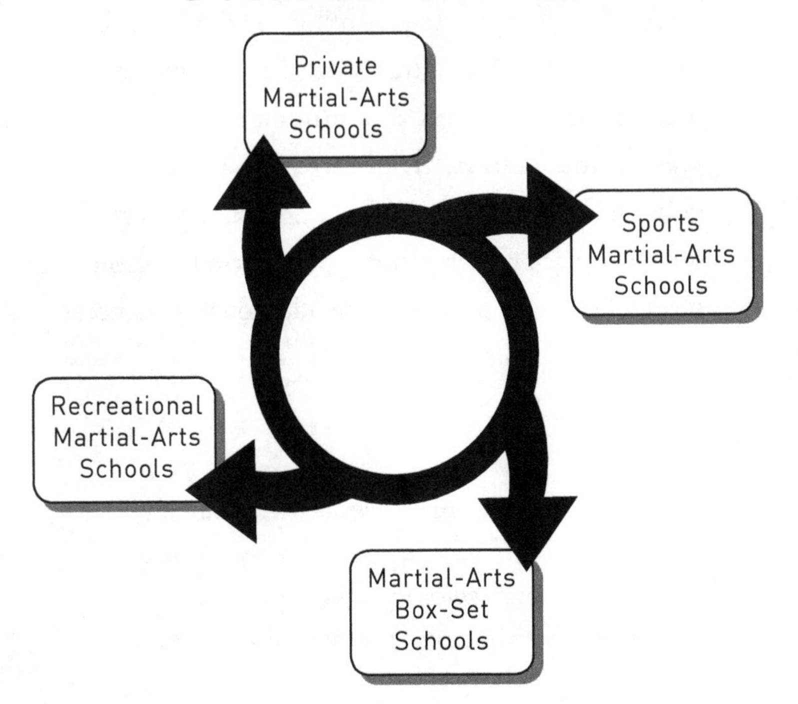

Recreational, Box-Set, Sports-Based, or Private School?

In my opinion, there are four genres of martial-arts schools: recreational, box-set, sports-based, and private school. Each has its pros and cons, and none is any better than the other. Some of the best programs have horrible people running them. Then, in contrast, some hole-in-the-wall studios supply devoted instructors and high-quality programs. To each his or her own; selection in such cases is just a matter of what you want or what you think you need.

The following is an outline of what I feel each genre of martial-arts school brings to the table for the practitioner. Again, this is based on personal and professional experiences that span more than thirty years in the industry. As a matter of fact, at some point in my career I have led an outreach program of some sort within each genre. I hope these first-hand observations will provide some additional guidance as to what would be ideal for you.

I have exposed my children to various sports, hobbies, and extracurricular activities since they were very small. When we discovered martial arts, I knew it was something that they would gain the most from. It's much more than just exercise or a sport. They learn discipline, self-motivation, leadership skills, and many other personal character traits that are important in successfully navigating through life. If you'd like to find an activity for your child that develops him or her in so many more ways than most organized sports, I whole-heartedly recommend a well-structured martial-arts program. The martial art teachers have given our children an outlet for exercise, fun, learning, and, best of all, character development. This is something not taught in school that they will carry with them for a lifetime.

—*The Whitehurst Family*

Recreational Martial-Arts Schools

Recreational martial-arts schools are usually located in recreation centers, gyms, churches, or other multipurpose facilities. For the most part, as long as you are a member of the recreation center (or facility), you can take classes. Recreational schools usually carry a significant advantage in terms of price because there is little-to-no facility overhead for the instructor. In addition, more often than not, the commitment levels are usually on a month-to-month basis. They tend to offer great programs for students interested in doing something as a hobby, in between sport seasons, or in connection with other related activities.

On a different note, these schools are located within recreation centers and multipurpose facilities. Therefore, such a school's environment can be loud and a bit chaotic, making it difficult to create the right learning environment. If you are not a member of the center in which the school is located, it is likely you will have to pay extra fees to participate in classes. In some cases, even if you are a member, there is an extra fee. Since there is less commitment all around, these schools usually have less qualified teachers who are, in some cases, students from other programs, or, in the worst cases, rogue exmembers of other schools trying to start their own programs. All such programs within recreation centers are subject to facility demands. So if there is a higher need, classes and programs will be moved, canceled, or eliminated.

How I Eventually Made My Recreation Program Work: In my early years of teaching, I tried to teach everywhere in order to generate more interest and serve more students. A few times, I taught in a recreation center. Each time was challenging, and attempt after attempt failed. It wasn't until I was approached by the city of Williamsburg to help with some at-risk kids that I decided to approach this type of teaching differently. Williamsburg's representatives wanted me to teach a limited group of students my program at the local recreation center. I decided to do it with one exception: the program would have to provide bus transportation and bring the kids to my school. I explained my previous experiences with attempting to start programs at recreation centers, focusing on how I had had little luck with truly making a difference.

After several discussions on the topic, the representatives agreed to a trial run. Now, five years later, the Williamsburg Youth Achievement Tae Kwon Do Program is still going strong, and many of its original members are still involved.

Participants of the Williamsburg Youth Achievement Tae Kwon Do Program at the 2008 Virginia AAU State Championships, with Program Director Master Joseph Ash (left) and U.S. Olympic silver medalist Mark Lopez (right).

Martial-Arts Box-Set Schools

I guess you could also refer to this segment as "fad" schools because they change emphasis to go along with the current trend. Workouts are full of energy and excitement. These schools tend to have the latest gadgets and flashy uniforms to go along with each particular training direction. Instructors are highly motivated and energetic when teaching, the music will be flowing, and students will be high-fiving their way around the class. There is a lot of great energy and flow, but...

The challenge for programs like this is that they offer little longevity. People who are looking for value beyond the kicking and punching will be disappointed. Fad schools tend to change appearances and location so frequently it can be hard for students to get a sense of where they are going or even if they belong. Again, these schools offer great workouts that have little content and that are part of a rapidly changing curriculum. Because there is no true martial-arts lineage here, most of these school owners actually do purchase box sets, or packaged curricula, and run such a purchase as the primary educational source. Of course, these programs come with a cost, which is transferred to you. Families that have been involved with such programs have consistently commented to me that they felt as if they were being "nickel-and-dimed" as they moved through the system.

• MASTER'S TIP •

I do purchase box-set curricula from time to time, but I do so for my own education. I am always excited to learn something new that could bring more value into my primary program. However, I would never use a prepackaged curriculum as the sole source of my students' education. Such a curriculum is like a box set of movies : you watch the set and find a takeaway, or not. Then, you put it on the shelf.

Sports Martial-Arts Schools

Sports martial-arts schools focus on the sporting aspect of the particular martial art. Whether it's tae kwon do, judo, karate, or mixed martial arts, the curriculum at such a school revolves around competition. These schools and the events they create provide another great way of bridging the gap between tradition and sports. Sports programs enhance fitness and do wonders for egos through hard training and competitive opportunities. Some high-level training programs can offer the best training facilities, best sport-specific trainers, scholarships, and even professional contracts.

Having the privilege to represent the United States on an international scale through sports was an honor that will remain with me for the rest of my life. The only thing better than that was coaching my stepson to the same level. Despite those experiences, today I feel many of the tournaments and related programs are losing value in their presence and doing an injustice to the athletes.

The author and stepson, Mitchell, after the latter made the AAU Junior National Team

I still run a successful tournament program and believe that there are many others out there, but overall, the people who lead such games (or competitions) and schools have greatly misconstrued the true lessons of martial arts. Students and parents alike tend to get wrapped up in the game or contest and forget the purpose of why they started. Even worse, when students don't win, they change schools, thereby creating a bigger gap among martial artists instead of better unity. Because these programs are so specific, they also can be more expensive than most, while providing fewer payoffs.

Private Martial-Arts Schools

There is a rising trend in martial-arts education: elite martial-arts schools are attracting more and more students these days. With challenging times at home, at academic schools, and at work, people are cutting back on average activities and turning to programs that have higher value and can provide greater personal and professional returns. Martial-arts schools that fall into this higher-value category are structured much like private schools: they bring greater value to the student body, which is mostly made up of families.

Through studying well-developed curricula, students gain far more benefit from their lessons. The staff and instructors go through formal training to ensure their methodologies are both consistent and practical for the various age groups of their students. The facilities at these locations are top-notch in both safety and overall comfort, providing an optimal learning environment. Such schools are also community pillars, providing a wide array of projects for people to work on together. Some schools even provide a pipeline that could lead to part-time or full-time employment.

Private martial-arts-school types are more exclusive, and some may wait-list students. Much like actual private schools, tuition for these schools will be higher, and students will have to make longer-term commitments. In the end, though, these are the most reliable and consistent programs out there, and they provide greater value and return on investment. Of all the benefits a good school can provide, character and leadership development is the one thing in which a private martial-arts school excels most.

• MASTER'S TIP •

In my opinion, having a school where lessons are structured appropriately and systematically so they produce the results of positive character and leadership is far more important than any medal, rank, or award. Today, more than ever, the world needs better people who will be better leaders, not just better gladiators.

Ten Musts for a High-Quality Program

1. A clear system for progression

The school must have a clear, somewhat predictable system for progression. This will both motivate students to do better and greatly help with retention. This retention helps maximize your investment.

2. Curriculum and/or support tools

There must be a way for the student to practice what lessons or skills need to be learned. Whether he or she receives a manual or videos, the student needs to have support tools that will help him or her develop good training habits outside the classroom. This aspect of education also provides other family members with a way to take an active role in the learning process.

3. Consistent teachers and staff members

Investigating the staff and the teachers is critical in learning about the school and, ultimately, the lessons. There must be a clear and consistent message from student to student. If the staff members are always changing, there is little chance the school's message will remain congruent. More importantly, if the teachers are regularly changing, it becomes difficult for students and parents to develop rapport or establish any relationship that would be conducive to growth.

4. A safe and welcoming environment

In addition to providing traditions, a school should have a safe and welcoming environment that provides students with a comfortable space in which they can acquire the skills and knowledge needed for their growth and development. Some key things to look for are the following: a clean and well-lit facility, matted floors in the main practice hall, a clutter-free training floor, new and/or current training equipment, and properly displayed signage.

5. Ongoing community involvement

Giving back to the community is a part of human nature, and such a quality should be part of a school's mission. After all, a martial-arts school is supposed to be providing a service to the community. So, look for the school's connections to local charities and participation in other community events.

6. Some sort of trial period or starter course

The school should always offer an opportunity for potential students to try out the program. Usually, these trials are free; if not, they are low in cost and commitment.

7. Higher levels of opportunities for education

Much like the ranking system, the school must provide an opportunity for higher education. Examples of higher education programs include the Black Belt Club, the Masters' Club, and the Leadership Team.

8. Instructor training program

Instructors must continue practicing and growing. How else can you, or they, expect to bring the students the best and most current methodologies in communication and education?

9. Raving fans

No program can be that great if nobody is talking about it. Ask around for opinions and hear what others have to say.

10. Flexible yet predictable schedules

Attending class two to three days per week is highly recommended, but that can be difficult if the school's schedule changes monthly. A good schedule is flexible in that there are a variety of options for attending weekly, so if you miss a class, there is a make-up opportunity. I usually only make changes to my schools' schedule twice a year: once for summer and once for the academic year. This is when I find families need time changes.

CHAPTER 3

MARTIAL-ARTS EDUCATION: VALUES AND COMMITMENTS

Martial Arts education has been an excellent resource for our children. Each instructor seems to care genuinely about the welfare and progress of each student, and the quality of instruction is always outstanding. Our boys have grown steadily in strength, confidence, and self-esteem through their participation. Overall, martial arts has been one of the most worthwhile investments we have made for our children.

—*The McWilliams Family*

How Much Does It Cost?

Inevitably, when you, or your child, starts at a new school, you will need to ask this question. For some, there will be no emotional charge; others, perhaps, will get sticker shock. The price for training fluctuates from school to school based on several factors, many of which are discussed in this book. I encourage you to take a look at the whole picture and consider what the school brings to the table. After all, it's really hard to put a value on confidence, security, and peace of mind.

The Price of Lessons

When selecting a martial-arts school, it's important to understand the decision is not like buying clothes or a television. There are all sorts of varieties and variables that really can determine a price, but to start with that question is a bit difficult. There is, without a doubt, a price point for everyone. What each person feels is the value of such services is the question. However, without knowing the services you are looking for, how can you determine their maximum value?

If someone calls me and starts the conversation by asking the pricing question, that tells me that the caller either is not sure what else to ask or is price shopping. If the caller is not sure, it is my job to help him or her by asking some more valuable questions in return (see the question chart at the end of the chapter). Price shoppers are easier for me to manage because I do not bargain. The situation is what it is: I have seen the life changes my school has made for so many that I do not want to undervalue its importance. In the cases of most schools, there is still such a broad array of skills, talents, styles, and services that it is virtually impossible to answer such a question, especially over the phone.

Most of us have had the experience of choosing the lowest-priced item only to have it cost more later. In regards to purchasing lessons at a martial-arts school, I recommend you think in terms of investment. What you determine as a worthy investment will, most likely, directly correlate to the set of values you have predetermined the program is worth. Predetermined value is also a big hurdle; it brings up what I call the when-we-were-little issues: something was such and such a price when we were little. I could on and on about this one, but the gist of it is simple: whatever it was (or cost) back then is not what it is (or costs) now. There is more value built in to high-quality programs today than ever before.

Tuition never seemed to be an issue when we selected our martial arts school. After considering the interactions of the instructors with my son, other students, and other families, the decision was actually pretty easy. Now, after almost two years, my son is not alone in his quest to achieve the rank of black belt. His younger sister, mother, and myself are also just as involved in class and we are working hard to catch up to him.

—CHRISTOPHER K. MCLAIN,
FABRICATION SPECIALIST, NASA,
LANGLEY RESEARCH CENTER

In selecting a martial-arts school, to base your primary decision on the price would drastically impede your ability to experience the ideal school in which you are making your investment. Here are a couple of significant points to consider in this context: Why do people pay for private schools when public schools are free? What about choosing a car? Do people always choose Kia over Cadillac?

• MASTER'S TIP •

The better questions to ask here are:

- What value limit you would place on your child having the confidence to raise his or her hand in school or say no to peer pressure?
- What value and/or services you would receive for the price?

I have personally invested more than $20,000 a year for the past several years in my own education.

If you are looking for a hard number, Internet searches reveal that the national averages hover around $125 per month for a small- to medium-range martial-arts program. What most people do not know is that the quoted rates do not include other, imbedded fees. In addition to regular monthly tuition fees, you should also expect fees associated with testing for new belts and mandatory equipment purchases (such as weapons, sparring gear, and so forth). There also may be required association or seminar fees tied in to certain programs. All that being said, these things have their place; in the big picture, they help retain students for longer periods of time. This makes the most of your investment. Just make sure you inquire about such fees and hold the school's representatives to their answers.

• MASTER'S TIP •

If you find a program that you you really like but it feels as though it might nickel-and-dime you, ask if there is an advanced-level program in which fees can be rolled into the monthly plan, thus making it easier to budget for such expenses (this type of arrangement is advantageous for families).

It is to be expected that private-like martial-arts schools will value their programs much more highly than other schools. Believe me, such schools can back up the reasons for this increased cost, and if not, you will know quickly. I truly feel the difference is not because people are trying to gouge you; instead, in such cases, these schools simply carry an abundance of added value that is unmatched by the majority. Their price options allow them to provide some of the following benefits:

- They offer services and experiences that some of the lower-priced programs cannot.

Such services and experiences cost schools dearly, but they directly translate into higher value and more education for the students.

- The management can pay bills on time and keep the doors open for years.
- The management can take care of their staff and their instructors well enough to keep them around, providing your child with consistent role models.
- These programs reinvest in their schools and their staff members' education, allowing for growth, which translates into their members receiving the latest teaching methodologies and skills.

• MASTER'S NOTE •

I read an interesting article recently about Americans and eating out. It stated that the average American eats at a restaurant between four and five times per week. This equates to $232 per month for that one person versus $58 a month if that person only ate out once a week. So here is the real, related question: What are you spending your money on that you could use to add more value to your life?

Commitments

Once you understand the pricing structure of a school, then there is the agreement to handle. Business people like you have bills too, and I guarantee the schools' bills are much higher than yours. Just the concept of a corporation can raise the price on items such as utilities and interest rates as much as 300 percent. As a result, you must expect some sort of agreement within your research for a school. After all, how can the school's management pay rent, teachers' salaries, and enormous amounts of taxes without any commitment from their students?

Let me say my piece about commitment. Do it! There is a great deal of value that can be added to people's lives with a bit more commitment and follow-through. As a parent, I feel it is imperative to have my children follow through on what they say. When they were younger and I felt a program was of value for them, I said yes for them. That is what a parent is supposed to do. Would you permit your son to act on his desires if he woke up one day and said he wanted to stop third grade? Of course not. So, why allow your child or children to stop doing other things? I am not considering martial arts now; instead, I am moving on to an extremely valuable life skill that needs a readjustment.

I am 100 percent behind stopping a poorly run program whose management has overpromised and underdelivered. However, the fact remains that too many parents cave in too soon and allow their children to stop pursuing extracurricular activities. Then they wonder why their children rebel as teenagers. The teens rebel because they have too much freedom to do what they want when and with whom they want. That has not done our society any good. Parents need a strong support system that will help them align their children with the positive values they, the parents, wish to instill in their offspring. This is the greatest service a high-quality martial-arts school can give families.

Grace and Sydney, friends forever

My First Lesson with Commitment

I was nine and had been training in martial arts for two years. One day, I told my parents I was done with tae kwon do and wasn't going any more. My mom calmly drove my father to the shipyard for work and then headed, with me in tow, to the martial-arts school. I told her I didn't want to go. After we arrived, she parked and gave me a mother's look. As every kid would do, when receiving that look, I got out of the car. From there, my mom calmly grabbed my hand, walked me to the door, stopped outside, and said, "You will finish your commitment to your black belt."

The rest is history. Thanks to her, I'm still making it!

Next, what commitment terms can you expect from a school? Again, that varies from place to place. Most of the time, this variance is determined by factors such as the outcomes you seek, the services you want available throughout the education process, how many times per week you or your family members want to attend class, and, of course, how many people are involved.

If you just want to do something with your child in between other sports activities, then obviously you are going to look for a low level of commitment. A good place to start would be the recreational programs, but you should still ask around. If you are trying to help mold your child into a well-rounded citizen by providing him or her with a strong support system outside your family unit, then you should search for longer-term programs. After some sort of trial period that may span anywhere from a day to a month, you should expect to be asked to enroll in a regular program that will last between three and thirty-six months.

• MASTER'S TIP •

Unless you are taking adult classes on your own or you plan to take lessons with your child, or children, ask for a one-year commitment to the school after the trial experience. While a year is not a long time, it is enough time to determine whether or not the program is right for you and your family. Plus, you can always upgrade to a higher-level program that provides more educational benefits and opportunities at any time during the year, should you so choose.

CHAPTER 4
BENEFITS

Confidence	Respect	Leadership
Community	Discipline	Friendships
Self-Control	Citizenship	Courtesy
Indomitable Spirit	Perseverance	Integrity

And so much more ...

How Is My Family Going to Benefit from This Experience?

Many books could be written on the benefits that may be gained from martial-arts education. Choosing a martial-arts school should always begin with this topic. Ask yourself the following questions: How do I want my child and/or family members to benefit from this experience? What is it that I want to gain from this experience? What can this program give my child, or children, that will be worth my investment?

The answer we all want to hear is that martial-arts training will give its students positive character and leadership traits. But does martial arts really do that? My answer would be yes. Face it. Everyone could benefit from consistent exposure to a program that continuously fosters physical and psychological growth and development. A parent needs to condition and expand his or her leadership skills. In turn, a child needs a strong support system that reinforces the character traits his or her parents are teaching at home: respect, courage, discipline, health, and citizenship.

No matter the endeavor, we should begin with the end in mind. Our goal, for example, was to find a school where building self-confidence was a focus, not just skill development. Know your goal before you begin your search for a martial-arts school, and you will find a school that aligns with the aspirations of your family.

—Jeff Carroll,
Assistant Principal,
Lafayette High School

The instructors at a professional school will provide all this and more. They excel at providing educational experiences that furnish considerable contributions to the growth and development of every student. These contributions go well beyond the techniques used in traditional kicks and punches. The only real way to determine if a program and its instructors have such a capacity is to interview the owner or leader of the school, and then try out some classes.

In all cases, regardless of style, the values or benefits must be one of the highest determining factors when deciding what school you or your child will attend. The instructors at truly professional schools will always aim to serve the martial-arts practitioner in ways that better the student's individual character. Character traits are what make people good or bad. In times like these, there is a much higher need for a good person than another world champion. After all, people who have values that are congruent with cohesive family bonds, positive citizenship, and overall leadership are those who are going to make a true difference in our future.

At schools where instructors focus primarily on physical matters or techniques, the curriculum will only capture one side of the spectrum. This is what I call the "martial way." More often than not, these schools have a hard time keeping students for long periods and struggle to keep the doors open. For a student, obtaining a skill such as kicking or punching only takes mental know-how and a little guidance. To be great, a student needs to transcend and find a higher purpose. This purpose, which is greater than the self, begins with the self, and this beginning also needs guidance.

To find such guidance, look for systems within a program that are going to provide the practitioners with true character-related lessons. Find out how these lessons are implemented and what related progression measurements are used. The answers to such questions will tell you whether or not the leaders of a school will do what they say.

Some helpful, beneficial ideas to look for in a school include, but are not limited to, the following concepts:

Structure and Discipline

It is traditional to have both structure and discipline in all programs, but more often than not, this tradition is a forgotten cause. Discipline needs to be viewed more as a code of conduct than corporal punishment, such as push-ups or laps. There must be a harmonious balance between discipline and activity at a martial-arts school. Such a balance brings about a certain element of what I call structured fun. This is like a fine watch that has hundreds of complex mechanisms running in sync with one another, creating a natural flow.

Respect

Starting with good, old-fashioned manners is a must for all programs. Terms such as "sir" and "ma'am" were staples of our parents' generation, and with them, these terms carried an element of perceived value in an individual. I feel our times have lost that quality, which is why many good children get a bad rap or are deemed guilty by association or through societal labeling. Most schools have such old-fashioned mannerisms already built into their cultures as a form of respect. I would be wary of those that do not.

Bowing is another form of showing respect in many martial-arts schools. Sometimes parents and teachers alike confuse bowing with a hierarchical action that is sometimes religious in nature. At my schools, the act of bowing is a mutual sign of appreciation for both teacher and student. From the teacher's perspective, he or she is thanking the student for being a part of the place of teaching. The student is taught to bow as an action of gratitude for the teacher's sharing of knowledge.

• MASTER'S TIP •

In some special cases, instructors may require bowing as a means of paying homage to ancestry or to some sort of hierarchical leadership. That method is fine if you are fine with it, but it is just better to know about such requirements ahead of time.

Focus

Often, kids do poorly in school because they just have poor focus skills, not because they do not understand the subject matter. Adults are the same: *focus* is a powerful tool that allows each person to concentrate on anything necessary to achieve a goal. The concept of focus is one of my musts for all high-performing martial-arts programs. As I see it, there are five areas of focus people need to master, and the sooner they learn them, the better.

1. **Focus Your Mind:** what you think and say to yourself become core elements of what you are.

2. **Focus Your Eyes:** what you watch and read has a direct effect on you and your beliefs.

3. **Focus Your Body:** physiology plays a huge part in your overall state.

4. **Focus Your Ears:** what you listen to drives what you say to yourself.
5. **Focus Your State:** what you believe and what things mean to you both drive your state of mind.

Confidence

Believing in oneself is an extremely beneficial outcome of attending a well-structured martial-arts program. Confidence is key in martial arts and in life, but how do we attain it? When looking up the word *confidence* online, I found that confidence is attained through systematically testing one's abilities to receive feedback on lessons learned. It is very important to see and feel progress. Many people start and stop traditional gym programs because they lose sight of their goals or they feel no progress. Martial-arts students periodically receive feedback on the effort they put into their training. Such feedback can be in the form of attending a teacher-student conference, achieving new belt levels, or graduating to higher-level programs and even more challenging skills. The concept of I *can* becomes more truthful to martial artists and leads them to a higher sense of self-worth and achievement.

SPECIAL REPORT ON MARTIAL ARTS AND ACADEMICS:

Attention deficit syndrome is the most commonly diagnosed disorder in children. The National Institute of Mental Health has determined that 3 to 5 percent of all American children have this syndrome. In 2004 researchers conducting a study wanted to determine the effects of martial-arts practice on the academic and behavioral performance of boys with attention deficit syndrome. Some of the researchers' concerns included seeing if martial arts could reduce the subjects' maladaptive patterns of behavior (such as talking in class, interrupting teachers, and leaving their seats) and determining if learning martial arts could improve and increase alertness. The study included three groups of participants between the ages of eight and eleven. The first was a control group. The second was an exercise intervention group, and the third was a martial-arts intervention group. The boys in the third group participated in martial arts twice a week. Their schoolteachers then completed a behavior checklist each week during the twelve-week study. The outcome of the study showed that martial arts increased homework completion, academic performance, and classroom participation; decreased broken rules; and reduced the number of kids leaving their seats. In other words, the study showed martial arts had a positive influence on academics. The children practicing martial arts increased their self-confidence and learned how to behave appropriately.

Scholars have conducted many research studies on the correlation of martial arts and academic performance. These studies have shown that students who maintain a program and train in martial arts at least three times a week perform better on tests in language and mathematics than their peers, who are less physically fit. This research also showed that this type of physical fitness reduced the number of absences in school.

Another point to keep in mind is that martial arts promote discipline. The discipline taught in the martial-arts classroom is maintained in the school too. Students will enter their academic classes with the same attitude they take in the martial-arts classroom, respecting the surroundings and behaving in a mature, correct way.

Generally, the study of martial arts increases mental alertness and helps individuals focus patiently and stay on task. Martial-arts practitioners respect their peers and behave within boundaries. They display less antisocial behavior including bullying. Martial art students do not miss classes as they did before starting to practice martial arts. The patience that their training builds helps them with studying, and thus they achieve better grades. Overall, the psychological benefits of martial-arts training help individuals commit to homework, focus their attention in class, and follow rules. These benefits lead to success and good grades.

Character development and leadership training, not style, should be at the top of each parent's list when searching for the right martial-arts school. A positive environment and professional instructors, combined with the proper education, will not only positively impact children's academic performance but will also provide children with the tools necessary to deal with future challenges.

Over time, several important studies have shown the positive aspects of martial arts, especially in the relationship of martial arts to academics. The following are the most important points:

1. Martial arts have been proven to increase homework completion, academic performance, and classroom preparation, all while improving classroom behavior and learning.

2. Self-control is found to improve among students who receive regular martial-arts training.

3. Martial-arts training is correlated to students experiencing greater feelings of inner security and becoming less vulnerable to attack.

CHAPTER 5

TEACHERS AND THE MARTIAL-ARTS CULTURE

Who Will Be Teaching My Child?

A high-level martial-arts program is more than a school or business; it is a culture. In such a culture, there are three consistent aspects: the teachers, the existing student body, and everything these people do together. The teachers lead the existing student body, the members of which, in turn, carry those lessons out into the community. Everything the teachers and students do together internally and externally affects the community around them, thus creating a culture that nurtures their core values.

Teachers

Evaluating teachers is of the utmost importance when it comes to selecting a school that is right for your child and your family. A martial-arts instructor can vary greatly in both abilities and rank. I recommend disregarding rank and accolades for a moment to focus more on the instructor as a person and his or her ability to connect with students.

First, I feel it is important for everyone to understand that martial art teachers are human and make mistakes like everyone else. They also carry a huge amount of responsibility, wisdom, and heritage that often creates an element of mysticism. Such characteristics can create a gap between certain teachers and their students.

That being said, it is very important to understand who is going to be teaching your child. This question is a must, and it should be followed by a question regarding how that person became a teacher at that particular school. Is the teacher another kid or a well-trained instructor?

I am not saying other students cannot help out with various aspects of a class; instead, I am emphasizing that they should not be running full classes all by themselves. In the past, the student with the highest belt would just jump out and blindly start leading the class in the instructor's absence. While some progress might be made in such a situation, I recommend that you look for a more professional program that has a true leader who is trained.

Returning to rank: I believe in disregarding rank and accolades for a few reasons. One reason is that the average person has little or no idea what that rank means or even if that rank is real. It is not hard, especially these days, to print off a certificate and buy a belt from an online vendor. However, a good indicator of someone with true rank would be a certification from the governing body of that particular school's system.

You may have to do a bit of research to acquire such knowledge, but if the end result is important to you, doing so will be worth your while. Plus, such information should not be that hard to find these days, with the availability of resources on the Internet. You just have to find out what organization the school's instructors are connected to and go from there.

Awards, medals, and other related accolades are another touchy topic. Sometimes these things are used as props to capture people's attention, but they bring no real value to the actual program other than bragging rights. Now, there are several champions in the world. If finding a champion to learn from interests you, go for it. Even then, though, how would you truly know the validity of an instructor's accomplishments, especially if he or she is from overseas? If you want that type of credential in an instructor, make sure to do your homework.

In the end, when considering rank and accomplishments won, such achievements really only serve the individual who earned them. Even though he or she may be a world champion or a tenth-degree black belt, achieving such a milestone does not mean he or she has any idea of how to teach your child or family members. Think of it this way: there are many academic teachers in the world who honestly passed their teachers' exams, but they are subpar when it comes to the actual act of teaching. The focus of your attention must be on the instructor's ability to relate to the student enough that each student gets the best education possible.

While the practice of martial arts has benefitted Grace in many other ways, we, as parents, feel that the most important aspect of her practice really comes from the amazing, masterful, and compassionate teachers she has. They have an amazing gift and ability to teach children, engage them, excite them, have compassion for them, and help them succeed in both their practice and their everyday life. In the end, without that, a school is just four walls.

—*THE GALINDO FAMILY*

• MASTER'S TIP •

If you are uncertain about things that come up in your interview with an instructor and want to do some homework, try a few of these avenues:

1. Ask a bit more about the instructor's background.
2. Ask for references and have each reference explain his or her relationship with the instructor.
3. Ask if the instructor is certified in first aid/CPR.
4. Check the school's status with the local chamber of commerce or Better Business Bureau in your area.
5. Check out the school or instructor on the Internet.
6. Watch the instructor teach a class.

Existing Student Body

As described earlier, a professional martial-arts school has a certain culture that nurtures positive character traits in, and learning experiences for, its students. In such environments, it is not uncommon to find students who have been involved for numerous years. These students are also great resources from whom you can gather information and additional support. I know in my own school the average student has attended classes for four years, but many are there well into their eighth year and beyond. As a matter of fact, I am now teaching the children of students with whom I trained as a young boy. It is truly amazing. All of these families provide great resources for new, incoming families. Joining in on such dynamics not only accelerates new students' learning but also helps them make friends for life.

Parents at a school you are checking are excellent sources for recruitment. They are the best spokespeople for any valued school. Parents are also a great source of support in predicting future experiences at a martial-arts school. They are essential pieces of the culture of a school.

Without a doubt, you must also interview the active teachers and school owner. From these interviews, you will capture their perspective of what it is they do. Plus, conducting an interview is an excellent opportunity for you to generate a sense of rapport.

It is very likely that one of your child's friends is already taking martial-arts lessons and perhaps has even invited your child to take a class. Such a class is an excellent opportunity for you to see first-hand how things are at a particular school. Often, when a child's friends are already involved in a program, that child's own experience is enhanced: having a friend at the school already eases the tension of starting something new, especially something mysterious like martial arts. In addition, it is always more fun to learn and grow along with friends and family.

Our family has had the pleasure of being involved with our martial arts school for over eight years. We cannot say enough about the expertise the instructors carry through all levels of the school, from introducing martial arts to toddlers to providing challenges and support to children and adults. The school and its instructors have been a positive influence on all three of our children, reinforcing discipline and respect.

– *Jack and Elisa Lemmon*

There is no doubt that not all people have the same interests. However, having a friendly referral or knowing of a highly recommended program at least guides you to a good starting point. I am sure you will find that even existing parents of a particular school couldn't answer all of my top-ten questions on the spot. (See Master's TopTen Challenge in Chapter 6.)

Community Presence

Every program contains classes in the school's form of martial arts. You must ask what else the school offers that can strengthen ties between the students, families, and the community. If you are searching for more than just kicks and punches, you will have to dig a bit further to find out if the school participates in extracurricular activities within the community. These activities create a wonderful connection between members and the community they serve. In addition, they nurture friendships and positive social skills, and they help develop a strong sense of community and pride.

It is very likely that a school of any value or sustainability has been around long enough to have established a strong community presence. Traditionally, as with most contributing businesses, a professional school will have an active, permanent community involvement. No school is complete without the concept of contribution.

Some great internal activities can include the following:

- school picnics/trips
- in-house parties
- private classes
- dinners/banquets
- special activities for specific programs
- testing
- guest speakers/seminars
- parents as coaches
- kids as leaders
- in-school championships

• MASTER'S TIP •

A school whose members act like a family and do more together, not just recruit new members, will take your family a long way beyond the curriculum.

Any professional martial artist will tell you what is done outside the classroom is just as important as what is done within it. Nicely laid-out and decorated facilities only help decorate the building. Go one step further and ask about community interaction. This will tell you the depth of the school. Ask about such activities in order to get a glimpse of how the school owners involve their members within the community. These outside activities are excellent resources members can use to recharge, stay focused, and establish a practice of contributing to something beyond themselves.

Some great community-related activities can include the following:

- community festivals
- school talks
- helping local charities
- fundraisers
- off-site seminars
- public functions

Not often are there times when the thing that you graduated from and changed you can become a partner to you in your trials in the days ahead. Very rare indeed are the times when the institution that changed you, from which you "graduated," appears again when most needed later in life, steps up, takes a leadership role, assumes responsibilities on your behalf and on behalf of the community, continues the process of growth beyond yourself, and expands into the areas most needed in the community. I can claim that honor of finding such a partnership, and I wish to recall with honor the service of Baeplex and Master Ash in the interest of justice in our community.

—LANG CRAIGHILL,
POLICE INVESTIGATOR, WPD

CHAPTER 6

MAKING THE APPOINTMENT AND TAKING YOUR FIRST INTRODUCTORY LESSON

My son was bullied in school and tormented walking around our neighborhood. I found a martial-arts school online, which he did for a couple of years but eventually stopped. I did not see any improvement and felt it was a waste of my money, even though you cannot put a price on your children's education. I found another school through a friend and have never looked back. My son's confidence and self-esteem is through the roof! He is now one of the school's assistant instructors, and periodically we get compliments around town about what a polite young man he has become. I can't say, "Thank you," enough!

—*The Wilson Family*

Setting Your Appointment

Truth be told, it is very hard to determine the quality of a martial-arts program from a phone call or outside a window. It is your duty to make contact and go and visit a school for an interview and/or tour. Again, investing in martial-arts education is not as easy as looking up the subject on the Internet, just taking the content there as fact, and buying into an unknown program. There is so much more you can learn about from visiting a school. You will benefit from the following:

- ☯ discovering the atmosphere and whether or not it feels right
- ☯ investigating the personality and professionalism of the teacher(s)
- ☯ learning about the condition of the facility
- ☯ seeing the actual product in action (watching a class)
- ☯ holding an interview and taking a tour with the teacher(s)
- ☯ having a discussion with parents who are on-site
- ☯ reading literature and other related handouts

This step is fun. Armed with some good insider's secrets, you will be sure to get answers to your questions and better understand what that school is about. Do not feel pressured or as though you must sign up right away when you visit. If the instructors or staff members make you feel pressured, then the school may not be the place for you. A good fit should feel right; enrolling should be an exciting, obvious next step. You should feel energized about the process as you transform from prospective interested party to client.

Once you get your appointment for a visit scheduled, use the answers you receive when asking my top-ten challenge questions to help guide your decisions.

MASTER'S TOP TEN CHALLENGE

1. What is your organizational focus?

Watch out if the instructor starts spitting out accolades about his or her own performance.

2. Who are the teachers?

Be wary if the management hires out teachers. It is hard to know which instructor you are getting and how long he or she will stay. Do the teachers participate in a regular training program?

3. Do you have a curriculum and/or lesson plans that the teachers/students follow?

Granted, you will be hard-pressed to find a school that actually uses lesson plans, but a belt curriculum that identifies what each student level should focus on is a must.

4. Do you have a trial program? If so, please explain it.

This trial can vary from a free, one-time lesson to a few months offered at a greatly discounted rate.

5. What commitment level can I expect after the trial?

Be concerned with one-day trials that lead to a three-year commitment.

6. What is the general price structure I can expect after the trial?

Every school should be able to give you a general idea or its lowest price tier.

7. What other fees can I expect to incur along the way?

Testing fees are normal but could be combined with tuition. This is less true of association fees, which some schools require.

8. Do you require students to compete in tournaments?

This absolutely should not be a requirement, in my opinion.

9. Is the school involved in the community? If so, how?

A school that is not contributing to the community is not fulfilling its purpose.

10. Do you have any references?

The instructor and school's references should include professional references, not awards, from any of the following: businesses, local schools, the local chamber of commerce, the Better Business Bureau, and students' families and friends.

YOUR INTRODUCTORY LESSON

Dear Student,

Congratulations! You are at the introductory phase of your martial-arts career. This is an exciting time for you to set your sights on how the program you have selected will fit into your life. Make sure to have fun and ask as many questions as you feel necessary.

On your first visit, try not to have any expectations regarding your performance. As a matter of fact, it may feel a bit awkward your first time. As a beginner, everything will be brand new, so just have fun with it. A great instructor will make you feel right at home through a delicate balance of learning, challenge, and fun.

What You Can Initially Expect

- If the lesson is one-on-one, it should last between fifteen and thirty minutes.
- A uniform can, but not always, be included. School representatives should tell you this prior to the first lesson.
- You will learn a few skills, usually two or three.
- You will learn mannerisms used in the school, such as bowing, answering, rules, and so on.
- You may have a little workout, which should be of easy-to-medium intensity.
- You may have more than one trial or be partnered with more than one other person.
- At some point during the trial, you should learn more specifics about the programs for which you have qualified, or are recommended by the head instructor or program director.

Most professional schools have either a specific introductory room or special times at which they host introductory lessons. This practice can be extremely valuable for beginning students who may be initially intimidated or overwhelmed by a group class.

• MASTER'S TIP •

If the introductory lesson starts on time, as simple as this punctuality may seem, it is an indicator of how the school's managers or leaders operate other areas of the business. The instructors should look and behave in a professional way that is representative of an ideal role model. It still puzzles me that some instructors will make phone calls while teaching classes. I do not allow my staff to even answer the phone while teaching.

During the first class, instructors should allocate enough time for you or your child to become comfortable and then to take away a lesson.

As the observing parent, you should also quickly note the general cleanliness of the school. Is it clutter-free? Are things placed safely away from the main activity area(s)? Watch and listen to the flow of the lesson. If you are not sure about things, politely ask for clarification. Remember the instructor is there to serve you, and if he or she doesn't know, you may lose out on a wonderful experience.

• MASTER'S TIP •

Observe a random class. Besides finding a good-looking school and a good introductory class, try and watch a bit of a regular class. Usually, this can be done before or after taking an introductory class.

MASTER'S OVERVIEW

Now that you have read so far, making a decision about your child's or your own martial-arts education will be easier. With the tools and information in this book, you can confidently interview, try out, and decide upon the ideal school for yourself, your child, or your family. Armed with the knowledge of how the martial-arts business works and the compelling questions to ask, you can feel certain that when you make your choice, it will be the perfect one. I sincerely hope you will pursue and find a valuable martial-arts program. Attending the right school will be a positive, life-changing experience and give returns well beyond your investment.

Use the review below to help guide you along the way in your decision making process fro a martial arts school. Feel free to contact me at **joe@martialartsunlocked.com** for any questions, comments or to simply share your findings along the way.

1. Choosing a martial-arts school should begin with how you want your child, your family, or yourself to benefit from the experience. A legitimate and professional program will be flexible yet predictable in fostering growth and development beyond the physical kicking and punching. Interview the teacher or owner and find out what the program's emphasis is and how he or she ensures the classes implement the values expressed. Remember that even though many programs claim to offer such experiences, they fall short on delivery. Be sure the owner or teacher can explain how values are taught from lesson to lesson.

2. Remember, martial-arts education is not a commodity product like a computer or TV. Therefore, schools can be very different. We all have had the experience of buying a less expensive brand only to find ourselves unhappy and, perhaps, buying another one shortly thereafter. Every person has a price that he or she can and cannot afford, but you should be sure not to base your primary decision on price. After all, the right school will bring a return on your

investment that is far greater than that of any educational institution. Consider what value limit you would place on your child having the confidence to raise his or her hand in school or turn down peer pressure when the time comes (and it will come).

3. Often, people call schools, looking for a particular style. Yet in reality, the style of martial arts taught at a school is not important. Face it. You heard of the style because of something you saw, read, or came across, not because there is an almighty style that encompasses everything your child or family needs. What is really important is that the lessons offered at a school are structured appropriately and make the experience fun, exciting, and educational. It is far more valuable to find a school that offers an emphasis on character traits and leadership training than one that offers whatever the media is hyping up.

4. Championship makes no difference. Do not base your decision about enrolling in a school on whether or not a teacher has won a tournament or specific award.

Unfortunately, there are many self-proclaimed champions and masters out there. Unless you are familiar with the entire organization awarding the championship and the processes for achieving that status or winning at that level, the topic can be misleading. What should matter in terms of a teacher is that he or she can connect to students in a way that ensures those students understand each lesson and its values, all while providing a comfortable learning experience throughout the educational process. Most of us have experienced this with academic teachers at some point: they can pass a test to be considered teachers, but can they really teach?

5. Be a wise consumer and take some time to talk with parents of children studying at the prospective martial-arts school. It is very likely one of your child's friends is taking lessons there or knows someone that does. Often, this connection also enhances your child's own experience as one of a group of friends who train, learn, and grow together. A well-organized martial-arts school creates a culture that

nurtures positive learning experiences. Within it should be a number of people on the same mission, and that in and of itself is a plus when it comes to raising a child.

6. Ask the school manager or owner about internal and external activities offered by the school. In addition to regular classes, internal and external student activities are excellent resources that existing members can use to recharge, stay focused, and achieve their goals. The bonding that is created through such activities further promotes a strong sense of community and pride.

7. Take advantage of a free introductory lesson. Doing so can be very helpful in determining if your child shows interest in a particular martial-arts school before you make any commitment. During the visit, take some time to inspect the school for cleanliness, safety, and security. Make sure the floors are well padded and the classroom(s) well lit. Observe a random class. Consider how instructors interact with students and how students react to instruction. In addition to locating a

good-looking school, you want to find one at which the instructors display excellent abilities in connecting with the students and parents before, during, and after classes.

8. There are classes and then there is everything in between classes. Besides class instruction, what else can a particular school provide for further education? Ask if that school has an actual system for progression, a curriculum and/or lesson plans for classes, on-line training in the selected curriculum, or some sort of at-home study guide. After all, a school should have some sort of measurable system. If not, how can you be sure you are going to get what you or your child wants or needs?

9. A professional martial-arts school should be structured in a similar way to a private educational institution. There should be various levels of the curriculum—beginning, intermediate, and advanced—held at various lengths of time and according to various tuition rates. At some point in the introductory process, you

should receive an explanation about all the particulars of that school's enrollment. Be sure to ask as many questions as needed. Representatives of the best schools will provide you with several support tools during this process. All of these answers are excellent resources you can use to help yourself make the best decision.

10. Some schools cater to the masses and let everybody in, similar to recreation centers. That means there will be lots of people, the atmosphere will be somewhat chaotic, and you will really never know who the teacher will be. You may get lost in the crowd. Fad or box-set schools change emphasis to go along with whatever the current hot trend is. These schools tend to change appearances, and sometimes locations, frequently. It is hard to get a sense of where you really are going or if you belong at all. Although the workouts can be great, there is a great deal of instability within these programs. Private martial-arts schools are more exclusive and may have waiting lists for enrollment. Similar to actual private schools, their tuition will be

higher, but the return on your investment is unmatched. These schools are pillars within their communities, providing each student with several years of service and education.

About the Author

Joseph Ash has been in the martial-arts industry since 1981 and is a proud member of the National Association for Professional Martial Artists. He currently holds a sixth-degree black belt from the World Tae Kwon Do Federation and after a successful competitive career, Mr. Ash turned his focus to teaching. He runs two martial-arts facilities in Williamsburg, VA, where he resides with his wife and three children. His schools have been an integral part of the community, working against bullying in schools and contributing to community cohesiveness projects and countless local charities and organizations. Today his passion is more alive than ever. He has a strong desire to expand his knowledge and reach out in efforts to help each person find his or her way. He can be reached for consultation or coaching via e-mail at **joe@martialartsunlocked.com**, or follow his blog, **martialartsunlocked.com/blog/**.

Grandmaster Bae at a demo in 1985. Ridge-hand strike through five bricks into a full front split.

I would like to dedicate this book to my family for all the support and encouragement they have given me throughout my career. Thank you to the families of my community that continue to believe in me and my mission to develop the next generation of leaders. Finally, to my teacher and mentor, Grandmaster Bae. Without him and the help of my parents, I never would have graduated from white belt.

How can you use this book?

MOTIVATE

EDUCATE

THANK

INSPIRE

PROMOTE

CONNECT

Why have a custom version of *Martial Arts Unlocked*?

- Build personal bonds with customers, prospects, employees, donors, and key constituencies
- Develop a long-lasting reminder of your event, milestone, or celebration
- Provide a keepsake that inspires change in behavior and change in lives
- Deliver the ultimate "thank you" gift that remains on coffee tables and bookshelves
- Generate the "wow" factor

Books are thoughtful gifts that provide a genuine sentiment that other promotional items cannot express. They promote employee discussions and interaction, reinforce an event's meaning or location, and they make a lasting impression. Use your book to say "Thank You" and show people that you care.

Martial Arts Unlocked is available in bulk quantities and in customized versions at special discounts for corporate, institutional, and educational purposes. To learn more please contact our Special Sales team at:

1.866.775.1696 • sales@advantageww.com • www.AdvantageSpecialSales.com

Printed in the USA
CPSIA information can be obtained
at www.ICGtesting.com
JSHW012044140824
68134JS00033B/3254